Your first 100 words in

HINDI

A Quick & Easy Guide to Hindi Script

Series concept
Jane Wightwick

Illustrations
Mahmoud Gaafar

Hindi edition
Mangat Bhardwaj

McGraw·Hill

*New York   Chicago   San Francisco   Lisbon   London   Madrid   Mexico City
Milan   New Delhi   San Juan   Seoul   Singapore   Sydney   Toronto*

1 2 3 4 5 6 7 8 9 0   VLP/VLP   0 9 8 7 6

ISBN 0-07-146923-0

McGraw-Hill books are available at special quantity discounts to use as premiums and sales promotions, or for use in corporate training programs. For more information, please write to the Director of Special Sales, Professional Publishing, McGraw-Hill, Two Penn Plaza, New York, NY 10121-2298. Or contact your local bookstore.

Other titles in this series

This book is printed on acid-free paper.

◎ Contents

◎ INTRODUCTION

In this activity book you'll find 100 key words to learn to read in Hindi. All of the activities are designed specifically for reading languages in unfamiliar scripts. Many of the activities are inspired by the kind of games used to teach children to read their own language: flashcards, matching games, memory games, joining exercises, etc. This is not only a more effective method of learning to read a new script, but it's also much more fun.

We've included a **Scriptbreaker** to get you started. This is a friendly introduction to the Hindi script that will give you tips on how to remember the letters.

Then you can move on to the 8 **Topics**. Each topic presents essential words in large type. There is a pronunciation guide so you know how to say the words. These words are also featured in the tear-out **Flashcard** section at the back of the book. When you've mastered the words, you can go on to try out the activities and games for that topic.

There's also a **Round-up** section to review all your new words and the **Answers** to all the activities to check yourself.

Follow this 4-step plan for maximum success:

1 Have a look at the key topic words with their pictures. Then tear out the flashcards and shuffle them. Put them Hindi side up. Try to remember what the word means and turn the card over to check with the English. When you can do this, cover the pronunciation and try to say the word and remember the meaning by looking at the Hindi script only.

2 Put the cards English side up and try to say the Hindi word. Try the cards again each day both ways around. (When you can remember a card for 7 days in a row, you can file it!)

3 Try out the activities and games for each topic. This will reinforce your recognition of the key words.

4 After you have covered all the topics, you can try the activities in the Round-up section to test your knowledge of all the Hindi words in the book. You can also try shuffling all the flashcards together to see how many you can remember.

This flexible and fun way of reading your first words in Hindi should give you a head start whether you're learning at home or in a group.

◎ SCRIPTBREAKER

The purpose of this Scriptbreaker is to introduce you to the Hindi script and how it is formed. You should not try to memorize the alphabet at this stage, nor try to write the letters yourself. Instead, have a quick look through this section and then move on to the topics, glancing back if you want to work out the letters in a particular word. Remember, though, that recognizing the whole shape of the word in an unfamiliar script is just as important as knowing how it is made up. Using this method you will have a much more instinctive recall of vocabulary and will gain the confidence to expand your knowledge in other directions.

The Hindi script, also known as the Devanagari script, is quite easy to learn. Once you are able to distinguish individual letters and symbols and how they are combined, you will find that it is a logical and consistent system of writing. There are no capital letters and, unlike English, most words are spelt as they sound.

◎ The alphabet

The table below shows the 38 Hindi consonant (non-vowel) symbols used in modern Hindi. At this stage, it is better to glance at this table and then try to familiarize yourself slowly with the letters through the 100 words.

क	ख	ग	घ	ङ	प	फ	ब	भ	म
k	k^h	g	g^h	ng	p	p^h	b	b^h	m
च	छ	ज	झ	ञ	य	र	ल	व	श
ch	ch^h	j	j^h	ny	y	r	l	v/w	sh
ट	ठ	ड	ढ	ण	ष	स	ह	ड़	ढ़
T	T^h	D	D^h	N	Sh	s	h	R	R^h
त	थ	द	ध	न	क्ष	त्र	ज्ञ		
t	t^h	d	d^h	n	ksh	tr	gy		

Some new symbols have been added for sounds borrowed from other languages:

ख़	ग़	ज़	फ़
Kh	Gh	z	f

Traditionally, a "full" consonant symbol from the table on page 5 represents a consonant sound plus the short vowel sound *a*. For example, the consonant symbol क traditionally represents the sound sequence *ka* (*k* plus *a*). To write only a *k* sound, without *a*, you use the truncated form क्. This is *mostly* true in modern Hindi, but the truncated forms are not always used, particularly at the end of words. Hindi has many truncated varieties of consonant letters, but to keep this book simple, only the following have been used here:

क् *(k)*, न् *(n)*, प् *(p)*, स् *(s)*, ल् *(l)*

The Hindi consonant symbol र *(r)* can assume different shapes depending on the other symbol or symbols it combines with, such as:

र्ट *(rT)*, वृ *(vri)*, फ्रि *(fri)*, ट्र *(tr)*

Sometimes, two or more consonant symbols combine to create a conjunct letter. Many such conjunct letters are used in Hindi and some (क्ष, त्र and ज्ञ) have been included in the Hindi alphabet. To keep this book simple, we have used only one other conjunct – त्त, a combination of the "full" form त *(t)* and the truncated form त् of the same letter – in the Hindi word for "dog": कुत्ता *kuttaa.*

✔ Hindi has 38 traditional and four more recent consonant (non-vowel) symbols

✔ There are no capital letters in Hindi

✔ Many Hindi letters can be truncated and/or combined to make conjunct letters

◎ Vowel symbols

There are ten vowel symbols representing the ten vowel sounds of the Hindi language. (One of these vowel symbols, strangely, is *invisible*.) Vowel symbols can be added before, after, above or beneath a consonant letter – but the sound always *follows* the consonant.

Look at how each of the symbols is added to the Hindi letter क. Notice the position of the symbols in relation to the letter:

- ा (aa) and ी (ee) are put *after* the letter
- ि (i) is put *before* the letter
- ु (u) and ू (oo) are put *beneath* the letter
- े (e) and ै (ai) are put *above* the letter
- ो (o) and ौ (au) are put *above and after* the letter

ा	ि	ी	ु	ू	े	ै	ो	ौ
a*	aa	i	ee	u	oo	e	ai	o	au
क	का	कि	की	कु	कू	के	कै	को	कौ
ka	kaa	ki	kee	ku	koo	ke	kai	ko	kau

*Since the symbol for the short *a* is invisible, so the letter क by itself may be pronounced as *k* or *ka*. But *k* (without short *a*) is sometimes written as truncated क् as well. This is also the case with the other consonants.

◎Vowel bearers

If a vowel sound comes at the beginning of a word or after another vowel sound in a word, the vowel symbol is added to a vowel bearer letter, as in:

अल्मारी (अ + ल + मा + री)	साइकिल (सा + इ + कि + ल)
almaaree (a + l + maa + ree)	saaikil (saa + i + ki + l)
(cupboard)	(bicycle)

The symbol for short *a* is invisible, but a vowel bearer still has to be used at the beginning of *almaaree,* otherwise there is no way of knowing that the word begins with the short *a*. The vowel bearer letter changes its shape depending upon the vowel symbol it carries:

- अ carries the invisible vowel symbol for short *a* and symbols ा (aa), ो (o) and ौ (au) making अ, आ, ओ and औ respectively
- इ carries the vowel symbols ि (i) and ी (ee), making इ and ई respectively
- उ carries symbols ु (u) and ू (oo), making उ and ऊ
- ए carries symbols े (e) and ै (ai), making ए and ऐ

Other symbols

There are two nasal symbols – ˙ *(anusvaar)* and ˘ *(chandrabindu)* – representing either a nasalized vowel (pronounced through the mouth and the nose at the same time) or an *n*-like sound before another consonant (which can be *n* itself), as in *king*. Nasalized vowels in the 100 words are shown in the pronunciation guide by putting *ñ* after the vowel:

नहीं *naheeñ* (yes)   महँगा *mahañgaa* (expensive)

Pronunciation tips

Many Hindi letters are pronounced in a similar way to their English equivalents. However, you should pay special attention to the following sounds:

kh (ख)	Pronounced like the Scottish "ch" in "loch," or the Yiddish "chutzpah"
raised *ʰ*, as in *kʰ* (ख)	The raised *ʰ* shows that the letter is pronounced with a strong puff of air, like the sound made breathing on glasses to clean them.
T (ट), *Tʰ* (ठ), *D* (ड), *Dʰ* (ढ), *N* (ण), *R* (ड़) and *Rʰ* (ढ़)	These letters, written in the pronunciations with a capital letter, are pronounced with the tongue curled back and the underside of the tongue touching the roof of the mouth.

- ✔ The modern Hindi alphabet has 42 consonant symbols, four vowel bearer symbols, ten vowel symbols and two nasal symbols – making a total of 58 letters and symbols (including one invisible symbol)
- ✔ There are vowel bearer letters used to carry vowel symbols after another vowel or at the beginning of a word. Some combinations need special attention
- ✔ Some aspects of Hindi pronunciation are unfamiliar and need special attention

① AROUND THE HOME

Look at the pictures of things you might find in a house.
Tear out the flashcards for this topic.
Follow steps 1 and 2 of the plan in the introduction.

मेज़

mez

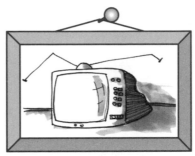

टेलीविज़न

Teleevizan

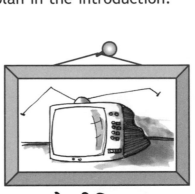

खिड़की

kʰiRkee

कुर्सी

kursee

कंप्यूटर

kampyooTar

टेलीफ़ोन

Teleefon

सोफ़ा *sofaa*

बिस्तर *bistar*

फ्रिज

frij

अल्मारी

almaaree

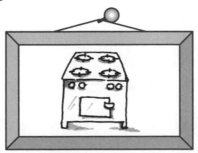

चूल्हा *choolhaa*

दरवाज़ा

darvaazaa

◎ **M**atch the pictures with the words, as in the example.

सोफ़ा
बिस्तर
खिड़की
मेज़
टेलीविज़न
कंप्यूटर
टेलीफ़ोन
कुर्सी

◎ **N**ow match the Hindi household words to the English.

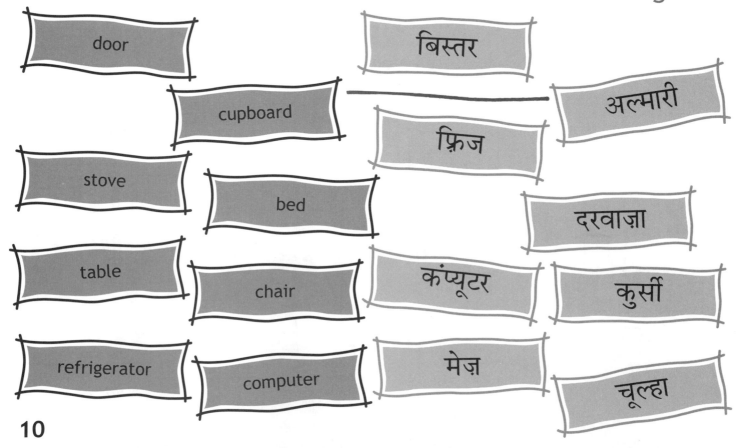

door

cupboard

बिस्तर

अल्मारी

फ्रिज

stove

bed

दरवाज़ा

table

chair

कंप्यूटर

कुर्सी

refrigerator

computer

मेज़

चूल्हा

◎ **M**atch the words and their pronunciation.

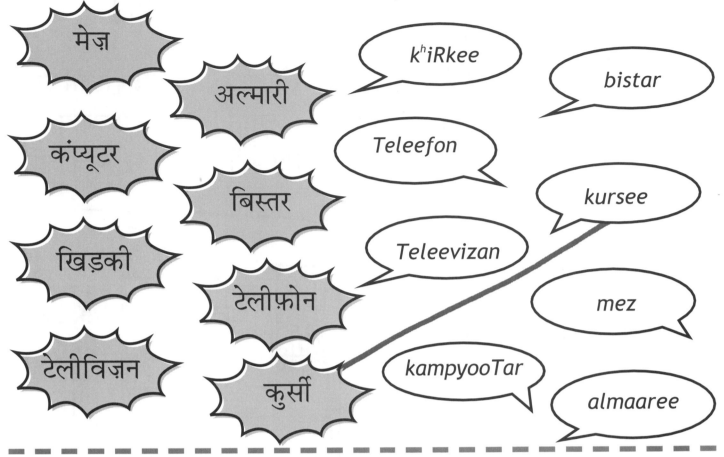

मेज़ अल्मारी कंप्यूटर बिस्तर खिड़की टेलीफ़ोन टेलीविज़न कुर्सी

k^hiRkee · bistar · Teleefon · Teleevizan · kursee · mez · kampyooTar · almaaree

---

◎ **S**ee if you can find these words in the word square.

The words can run left to right, or top to bottom:

बिस्तर
चूल्हा
कुर्सी
फ्रिज
दरवाज़ा
सोफ़ा

क	फ़ा	द	क	ट	कु	क्ष	फ्रि
सो	वा	ही	म	र	सीं	फ़	भ
द	सो	ज	बि	चू	ज़ा	वा	क
चू	ग	फ्रि	ज	म	सीं	ज़ा	र
जि	ग	र	द	र	चू	ल	हा
बि	र	त	र	ज	हा	म	ट
इं	ग	लैं	वा	वे	सीं	ज़	सो
द	फ्रि	द	ज़ा	वा	ज़ा	स	फ़ा

11

© **D**ecide where the household items should go. Then write the correct number in the picture, as in the example.

1. मेज़   2. कुर्सी   3. सोफ़ा   4. टेलीविज़न
5. टेलीफ़ोन   6. बिस्तर   7. अल्मारी   8. चूल्हा
9. फ्रिज   10. कंप्यूटर   11. खिड़की   12. दरवाज़ा

◎ **N**ow see if you can fill in the household word at the bottom of the page by choosing the correct Hindi.

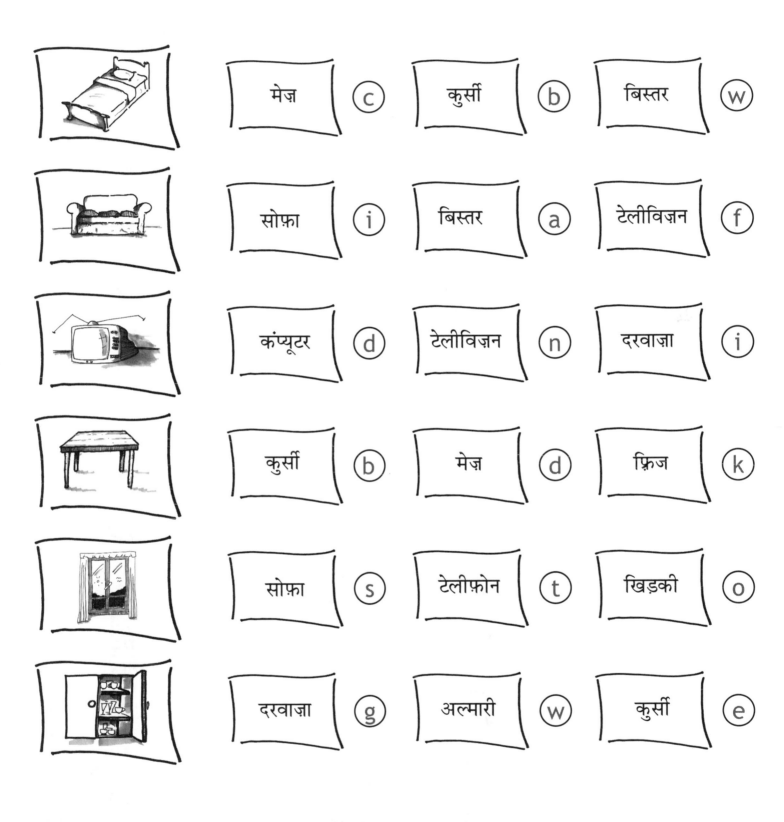

मेज़ ⓒ   कुर्सी ⓑ   बिस्तर ⓦ

सोफ़ा ⓘ   बिस्तर ⓐ   टेलीविज़न ⓕ

कंप्यूटर ⓓ   टेलीविज़न ⓝ   दरवाज़ा ⓘ

कुर्सी ⓑ   मेज़ ⓓ   फ्रिज ⓚ

सोफ़ा ⓢ   टेलीफ़ोन ⓣ   खिड़की ⓞ

दरवाज़ा ⓖ   अल्मारी ⓦ   कुर्सी ⓔ

English word: ⓦ ◯ ◯ ◯ ◯ ◯

② CLOTHES

Look at the pictures of different clothes.
Tear out the flashcards for this topic.
Follow steps 1 and 2 of the plan in the introduction.

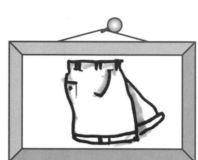

पेटी
peTee

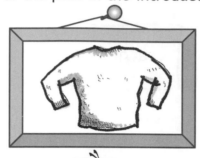

स्वैटर
svaiTar

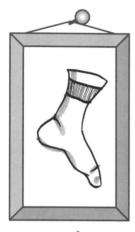

जुर्राब
jurraab

टी शर्ट
Tee sharT

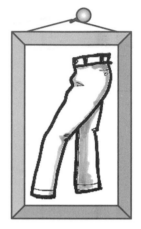

निक्कर
nikkar

पतलून
patloon

कोट
koT

स्कर्ट
skarT

ड्रेस
Dres

टोपी *Topee*

जूता *jootaa*

कमीज़ *kameez*

◎ **M**atch the Hindi words and their pronunciation.

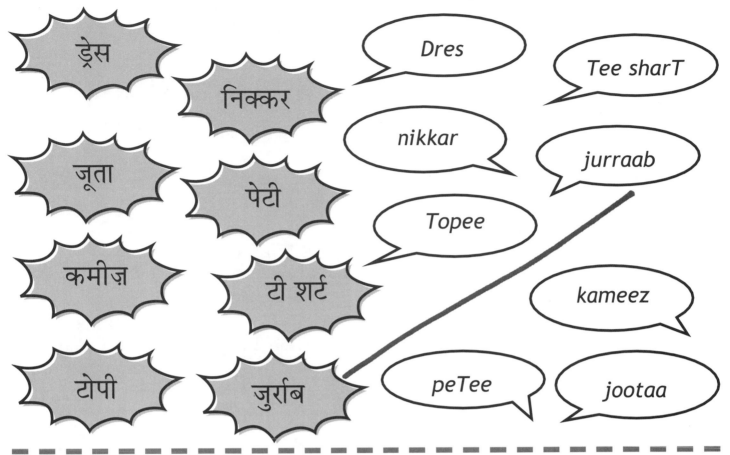

ड्रेस

निक्कर

जूता

पेटी

कमीज़

टी शर्ट

टोपी

जुराॅब

Dres

Tee sharT

nikkar

jurraab

Topee

kameez

peTee

jootaa

- -

◎ **S**ee if you can find these clothes in the word square.

The words can run left to right, or top to bottom:

को	ल	क	ड	जु	ज़	जु	को
म	स्	को	ट	म	त	लू	न
ला	र	को	नि	ता	जु	रॉ	ब
प	क	मी	क्त	ट	ब	ट	स
क	स	को	क	प	ज़	को	जू
स्	वै	ट	र	त	र	ष	ता
र	स्	क	ॅट	लू	टी	को	क
क	ब	स्	ट	न	म	को	प

15

◎ **N**ow match the Hindi words, their pronunciation, and the English meaning, as in the example.

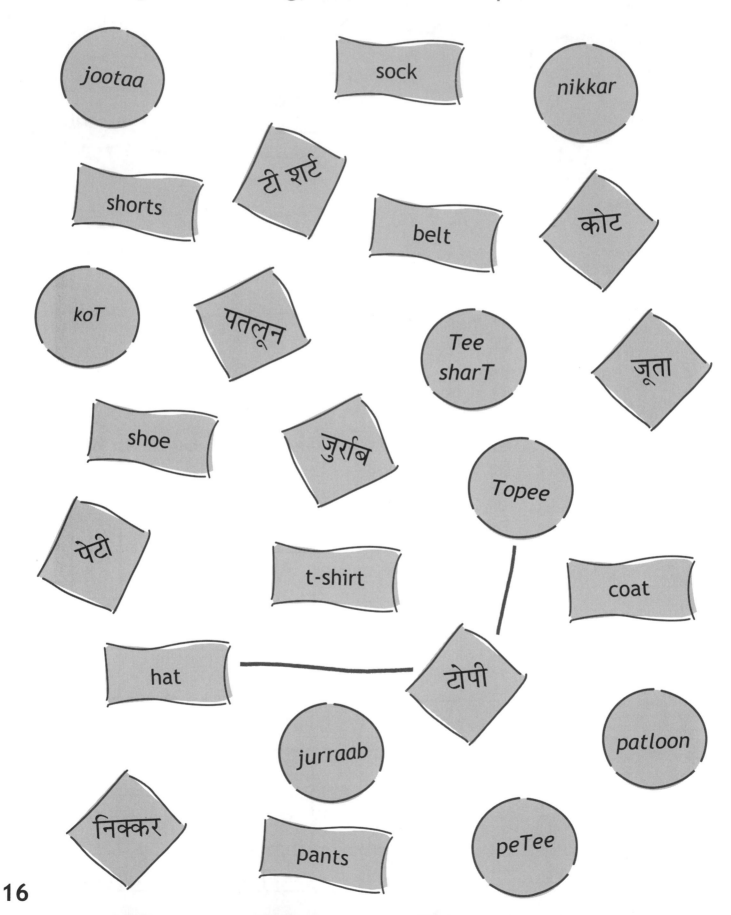

jootaa

sock

nikkar

shorts

टी शर्ट

belt

कोट

koT

पतलून

Tee sharT

जूता

shoe

जुर्राब

Topee

पेटी

t-shirt

coat

hat

टोपी

patloon

जुर्राब — jurraab

निक्कर

pants

peTee

◎ **C**andy is going on vacation. Count how many of each type of clothing she is packing in her suitcase.

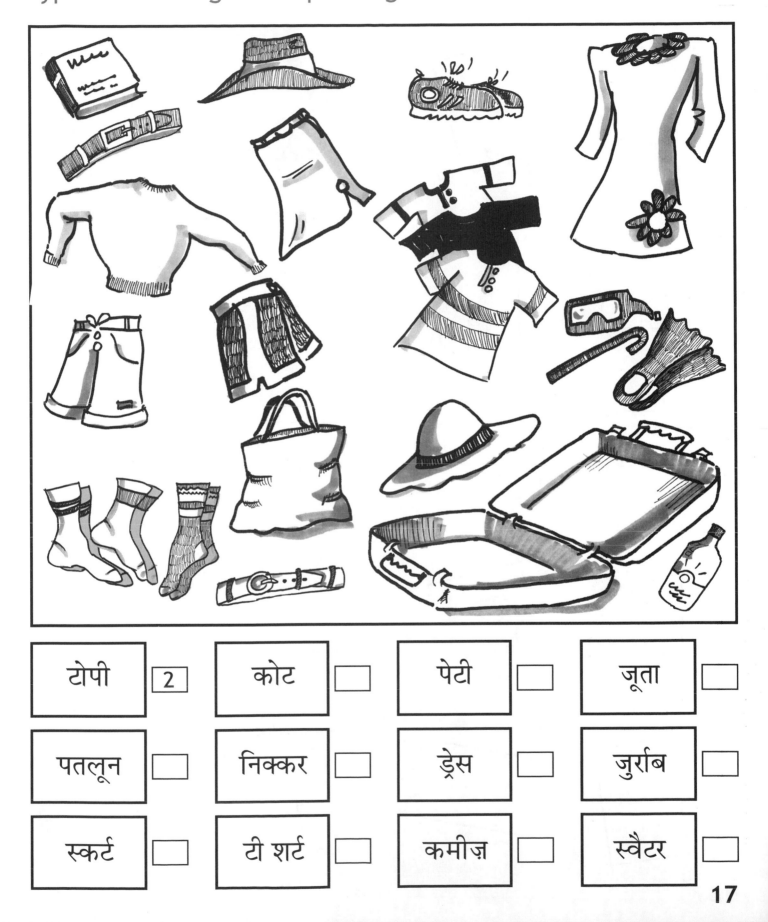

टोपी	2	कोट		पेटी		जूता	
पतलून		निक्कर		ड्रेस		जुराब	
स्कर्ट		टी शर्ट		कमीज़		स्वैटर	

Someone has ripped up the Hindi words for clothes.
Can you join the two halves of the words, as the example?

18

❸ AROUND TOWN

Look at the pictures of things you might find around town.
Tear out the flashcards for this topic.
Follow steps 1 and 2 of the plan in the introduction.

होटल *hoTal*

बस
bas

घर
gʰar

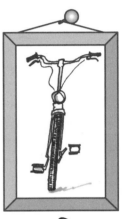

साइकिल
saaikil

कार
kaar

सिनेमा
sinemaa

रेलगाड़ी
relgaaRee

टैक्सी *Taiksee*

स्कूल *skool*

सड़क *saRak*

दुकान *dukaan*

रेस्टोरेंट
restorenT

◎ **M**atch the Hindi words to their English equivalents.

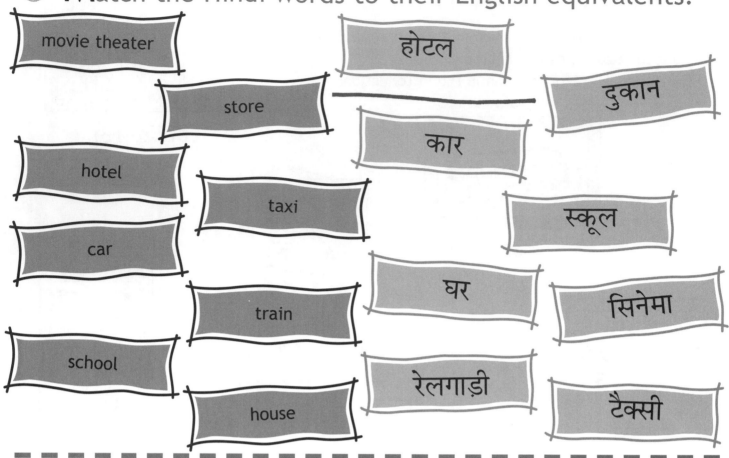

movie theater

store

hotel

car

school

taxi

train

house

होटल

दुकान

कार

स्कूल

घर

सिनेमा

रेलगाड़ी

टैक्सी

◎ **N**ow put the English words in the same order as the Hindi word chain, as in the example.

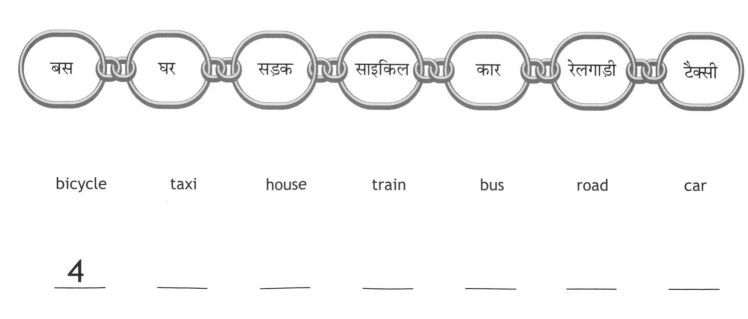

बस   घर   सड़क   साइकिल   कार   रेलगाड़ी   टैक्सी

bicycle   taxi   house   train   bus   road   car

<u>   4   </u> ___ ___ ___ ___ ___ ___

◎ **M**atch the words to the signs.

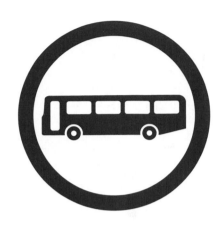

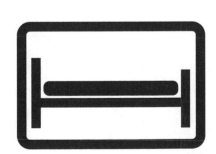

स्कूल	कार	साइकिल	बस
रेस्टोरेंट	रेलगाड़ी	होटल	टैक्सी

Now choose the Hindi word that matches the picture to fill in the English word at the bottom of the page.

टैक्सी c	कार f	घर s
सड़क c	स्कूल a	बस k
रेलगाड़ी h	कार e	रेस्टोरेंट u
घर b	साइकिल o	रेलगाड़ी w
स्कूल o	सड़क h	होटल s
होटल r	दुकान g	सिनेमा l

English word: s ◯ ◯ ◯ ◯ ◯

Now match the Hindi words to their pronunciation.

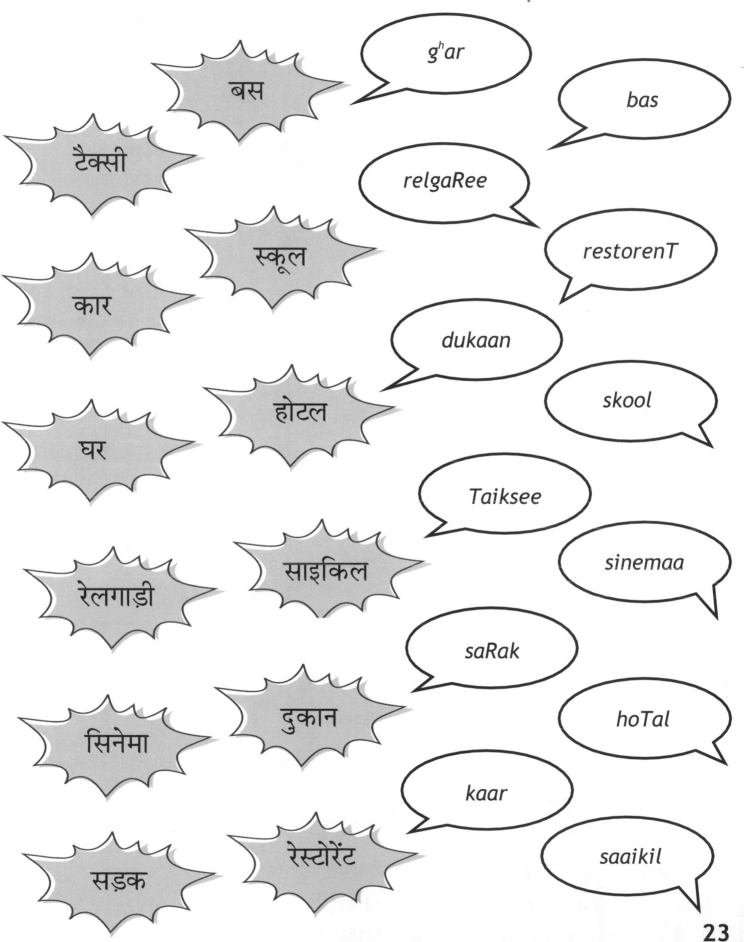

4 COUNTRYSIDE

Look at the pictures of features you might find in the countryside.
Tear out the flashcards for this topic.
Follow steps 1 and 2 of the plan in the introduction.

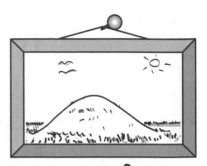

पहाड़ी
pahaaRee

पुल
pul

फ़ार्म
faarm

पहाड़
pahaaR

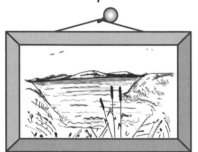

झील
jʰeel

वृक्ष
vriksh

फूल
pʰool

नदी *nadee*

सागर *saagar*

खेत *kʰet*

रेगिस्तान
registaan

वन
van

24

◎ **C**an you match all the countryside words to the pictures.

पहाड़

फ़ार्म

सागर

वन

रेगिस्तान

पहाड़ी

झील

पुल

नदी

फूल

वृक्ष

खेत

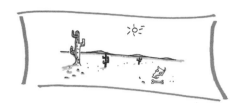

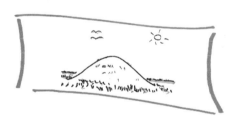

◎ **N**ow check (✔) the features you can find in this landscape.

पुल	✔	वृक्ष	☐	रेगिस्तान	☐	पहाड़ी	☐
पहाड़	☐	सागर	☐	खेत	☐	वन	☐
झील	☐	नदी	☐	फूल	☐	फ़ार्म	☐

Match the Hindi words and their pronunciation.

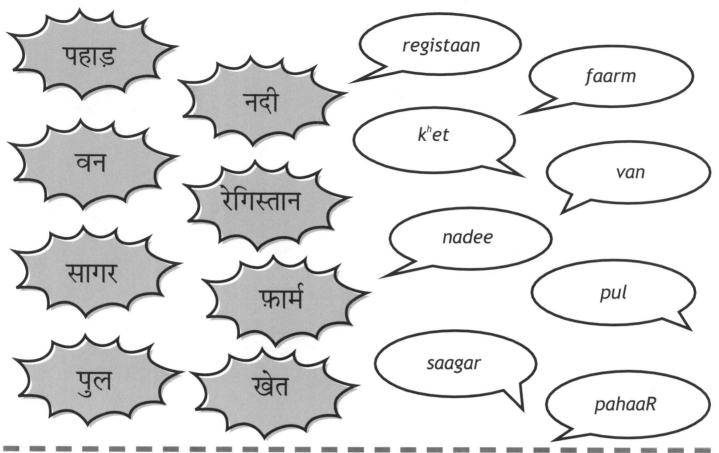

- -

See if you can find these words in the word square.

The words can run left to right, or top to bottom.

mountain

tree

farm

flower

bridge

lake

झी	म	क	ग	पु	फू	ट	स
र	पु	व	वृ	ल	झी	ष	क्ष
फु	स	फू	क्ष	ड़ा	ल	वृ	र
त	पु	र	श	भ	फ़ा	ख	झी
ट	र	ल	ला	थ	र्म	क्ष	पु
प	हा	ड़ी	लू	वृ	ल	फू	ल
ढ़	य	रू	झी	सी	व	ह	झ
.ढ	वृ	घ	झी	ल	ण	क्ष	थ

27

◎ **F**inally, test yourself by joining the Hindi words, their pronunciation, and the English meanings, as in the example.

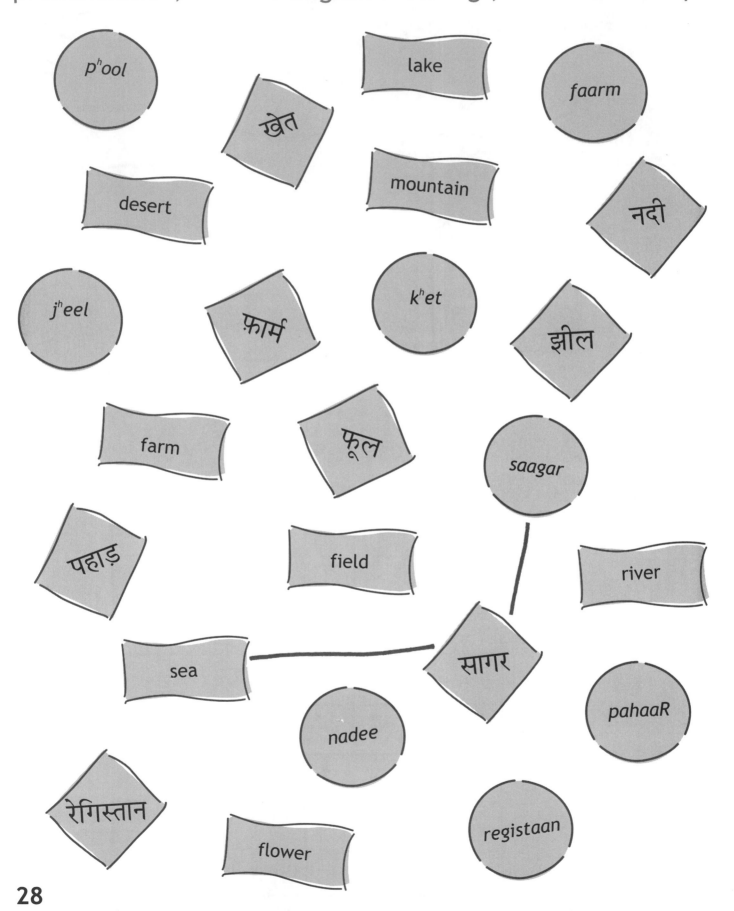

⑤ OPPOSITES

Look at the pictures.
Tear out the flashcards for this topic.
Follow steps 1 and 2 of the plan in the introduction.

गंदा
gandaa

साफ़
saaf

छोटा
chʰoTaa

बड़ा
baRaa

सस्ता
sastaa

हल्का *halkaa*

धीमा *dʰeemaa*

महँगा
mahañgaa

भारी
bʰaaree

तेज़ *tez*

पुराना *puraanaa*

नया *nayaa*

Join the Hindi words to their English equivalents.

expensive

साफ़

भारी

big

छोटा

light

पुराना

slow

नया

clean

inexpensive ———— सस्ता

तेज़

dirty

धीमा

small

महँगा

heavy

गंदा

new

हल्का

fast

old

बड़ा

30

◎ **N**ow choose the Hindi word that matches the picture to fill in the English word at the bottom of the page.

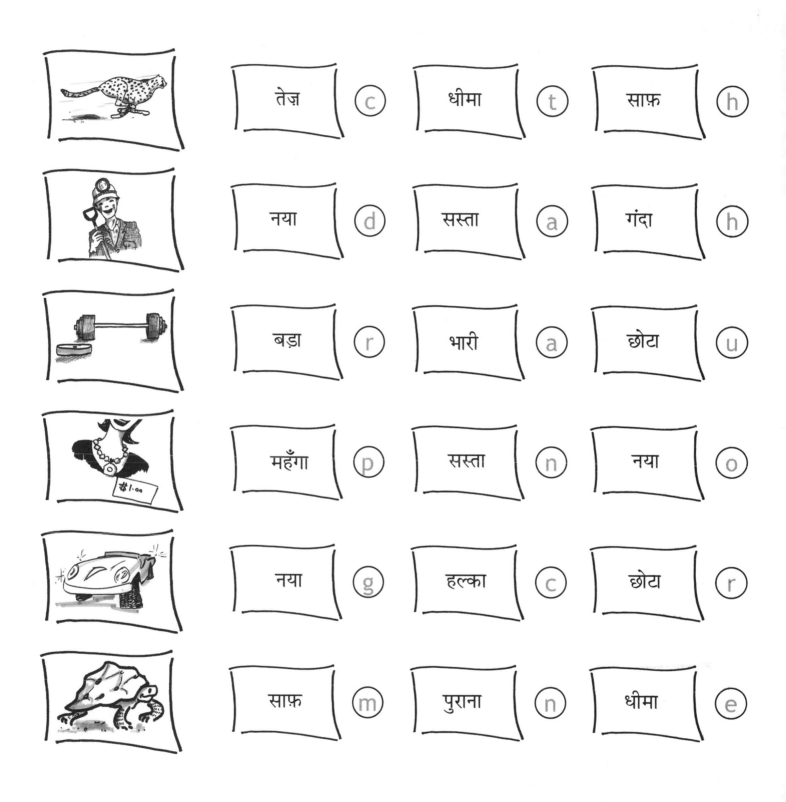

तेज़ ⓒ	धीमा ⓣ	साफ़ ⓗ
नया ⓓ	सस्ता ⓐ	गंदा ⓗ
बड़ा ⓡ	भारी ⓐ	छोटा ⓤ
महँगा ⓟ	सस्ता ⓝ	नया ⓞ
नया ⓖ	हल्का ⓒ	छोटा ⓡ
साफ़ ⓜ	पुराना ⓝ	धीमा ⓔ

English word: ⓒ ◯ ◯ ◯ ◯ ◯

Find the odd one out in these groups of words.

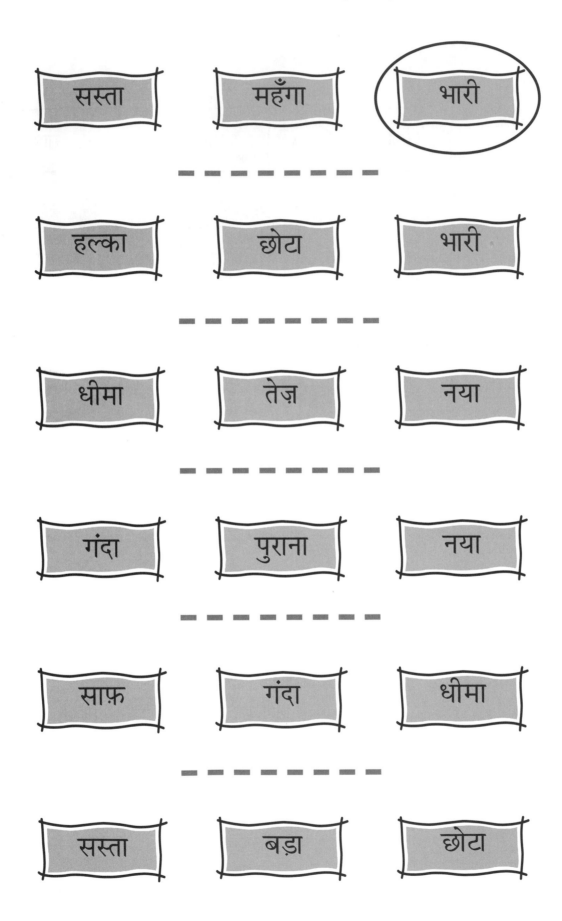

सस्ता	महँगा	(भारी)
हल्का	छोटा	भारी
धीमा	तेज़	नया
गंदा	पुराना	नया
साफ़	गंदा	धीमा
सस्ता	बड़ा	छोटा

◎ **F**inally, join the English words to their Hindi opposites, as in the example.

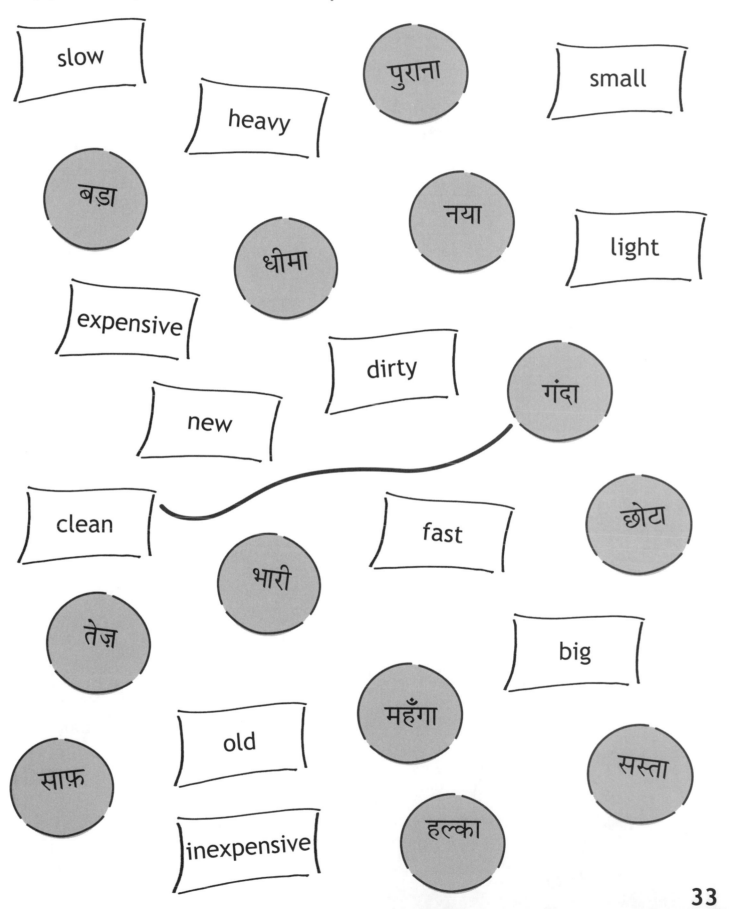

slow

heavy

पुराना

small

बड़ा

नया

light

धीमा

expensive

dirty

गंदा

new

clean

fast

छोटा

भारी

तेज़

big

महँगा

old

साफ़

सस्ता

inexpensive

हल्का

33

6 ANIMALS

Look at the pictures.
Tear out the flashcards for this topic.
Follow steps 1 and 2 of the plan in the introduction.

बत्तख *battakh*

हाथी
haathee

बिल्ली
billee

कुत्ता
kuttaa

ख़रगोश
khargosh

बंदर
bandar

मछली *machalee*

भेड़ *bheR*

चूहा *choohaa*

गाय *gaay*

घोड़ा
ghoRaa

शेर
sher

Match the animals to their associated pictures, as in the example.

घोड़ा

ख़रगोश

बंदर

बिल्ली

भेड़

चूहा

कुत्ता

शेर

गाय

मछली

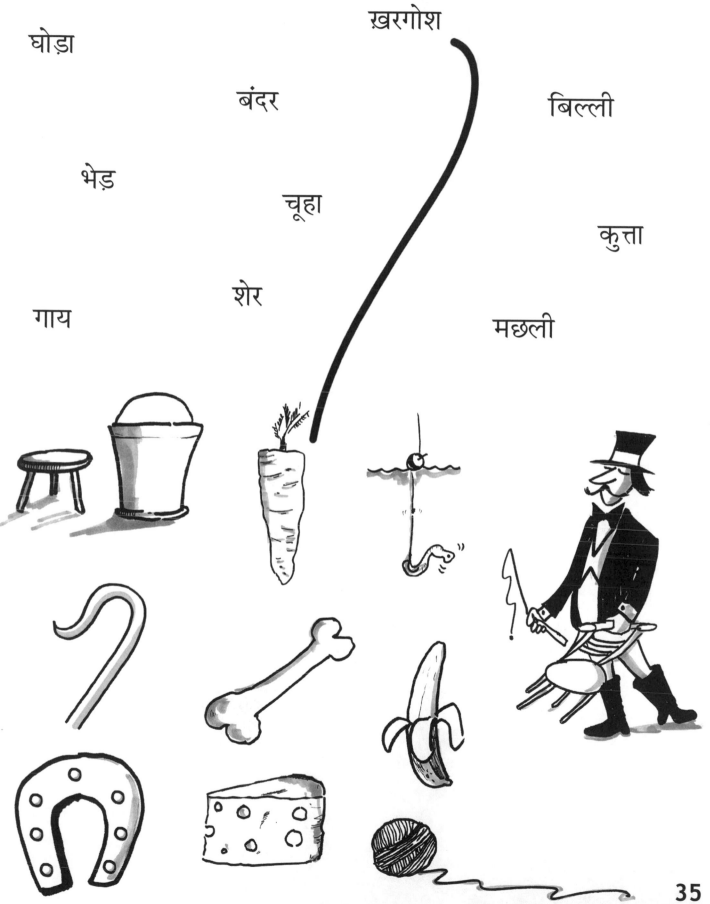

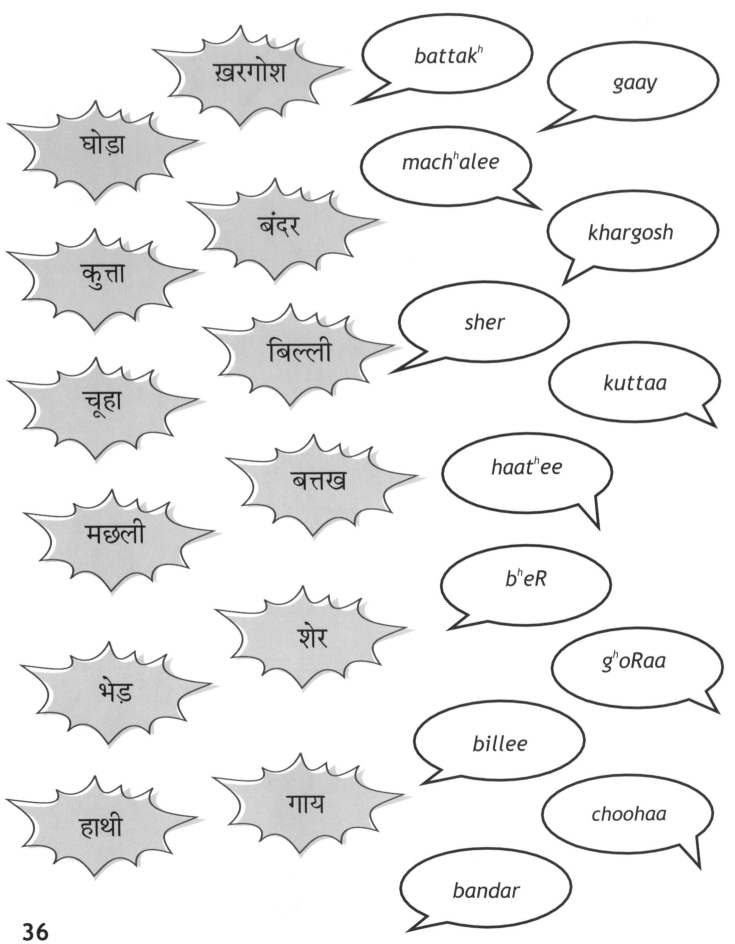

Check (✔) the animal words you can find in the word pile.

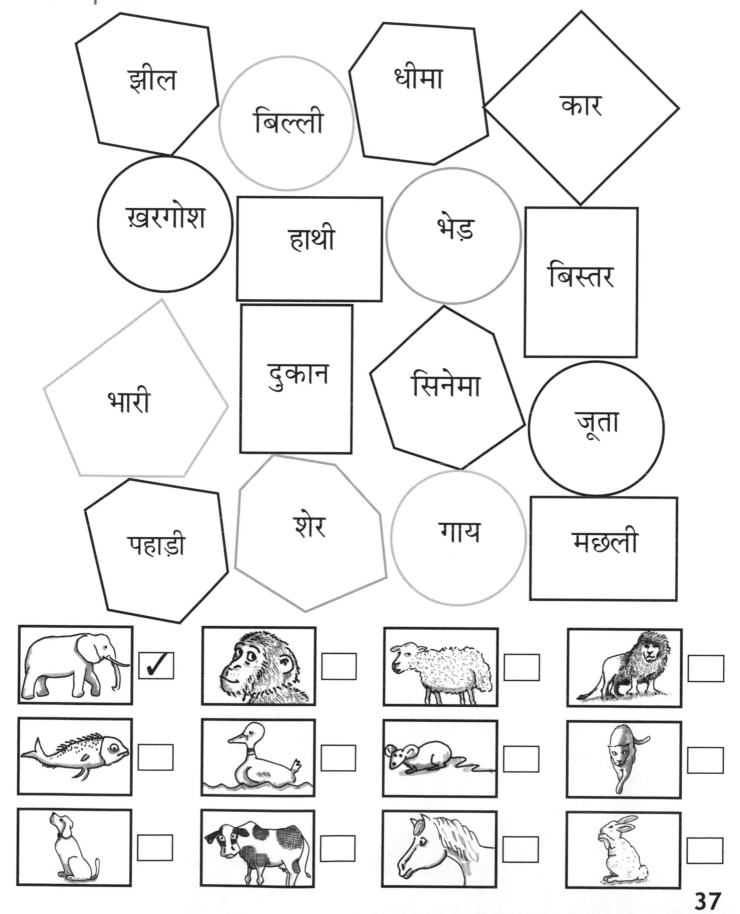

झील

बिल्ली

धीमा

कार

ख़रगोश

हाथी

भेड़

बिस्तर

भारी

दुकान

सिनेमा

जूता

पहाड़ी

शेर

गाय

मछली

Join the Hindi animals to their English equivalents.

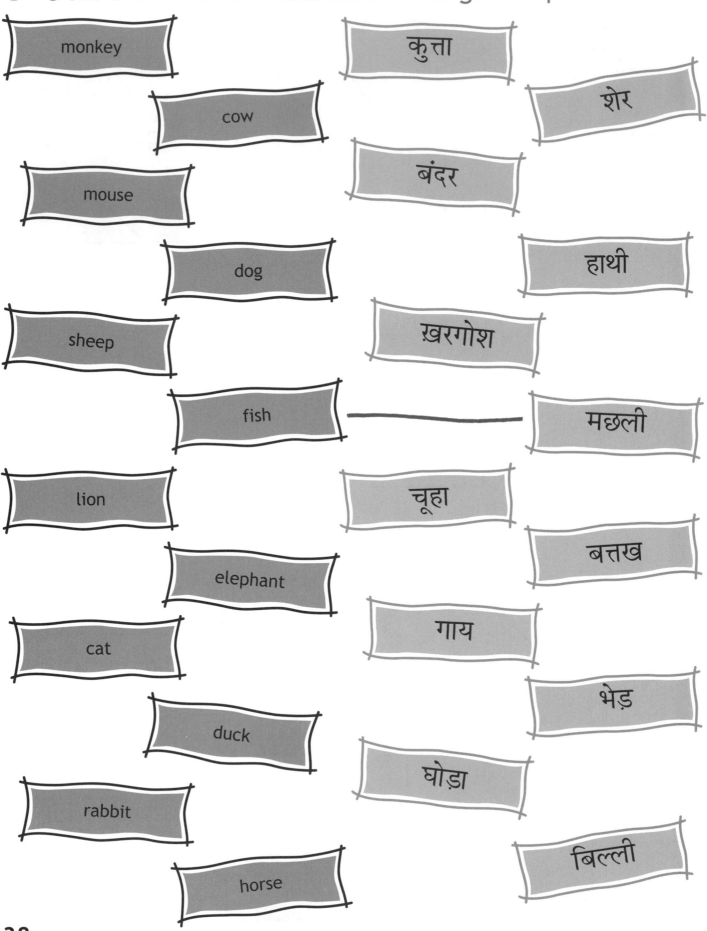

monkey

कुत्ता

शेर

cow

बंदर

mouse

dog

हाथी

sheep

ख़रगोश

fish

मछली

lion

चूहा

बत्तख

elephant

गाय

cat

भेड़

duck

घोड़ा

rabbit

बिल्ली

horse

⑦ PARTS OF THE BODY

Look at the pictures of parts of the body.
Tear out the flashcards for this topic.
Follow steps 1 and 2 of the plan in the introduction.

उँगली
uñgalee

सिर
sir

बाँह
baañh

आँख *aañk^h*

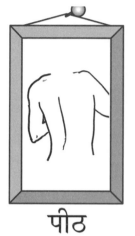

पीठ
peeT^h

हाथ
haat^h

बाल *baal*

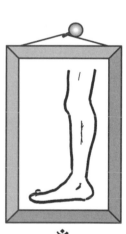

टाँग
Taañg

पेट
peT

कान
kaan

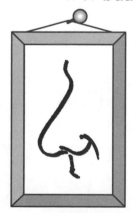

नाक
naak

मुँह
muñh

39

Someone has ripped up the Hindi words for parts of the body. Can you join the two halves of the word again?

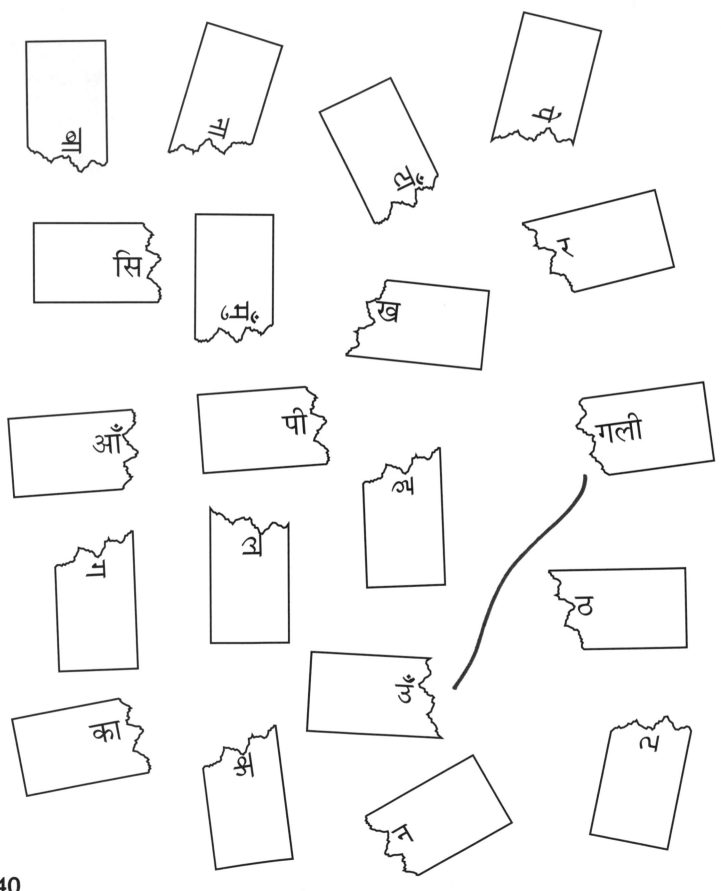

⊙ **S**ee if you can find and circle six parts of the body in the word square, then draw them in the boxes below.

म	स	ह	कि	च	झ	ड	ष
क	टाँ	ग	ढ़	व	टाँ	का	क
स	ह	झ	दो	मुँ	व	स	र
प	रू	मुँ	घ	ह	आँ	व	ला
घ	क्षी	न	य	ह	स	ली	बा
ठ	त	नृ	का	न	म	क	ल
ढ	आँ	ख	ल	श	क	र	पु
छ	थ	ना	क	लि	घ	ण	म

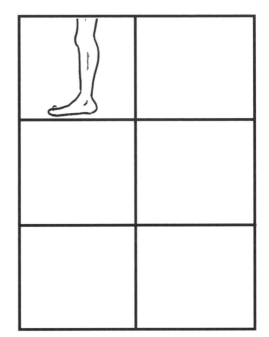

⊙ **N**ow match the Hindi to the pronunciation.

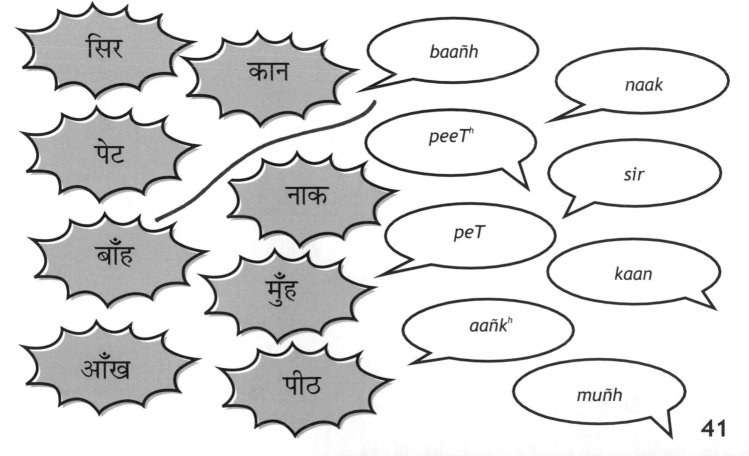

सिर   कान   *baañh*   *naak*

पेट   *peeTʰ*   *sir*

नाक   *peT*

बाँह   मुँह   *kaan*

aañkʰ

आँख   पीठ   *muñh*

◎ **L**abel the body with the correct number, and write the pronunciation next to the words.

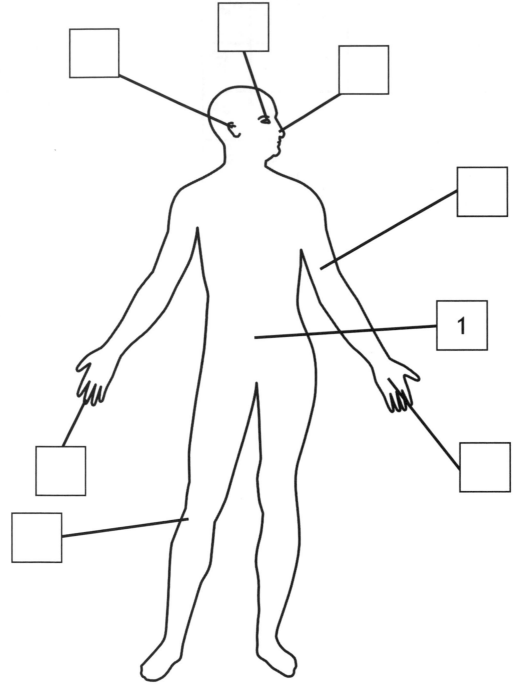

1 पेट   *peT*   2 बाँह   _____

3 नाक   _____   4 हाथ   _____

5 कान   _____   6 टाँग   _____

7 आँख   _____   8 उँगली   _____

Finally, match the Hindi words, their pronunciation, and the English meanings, as in the example.

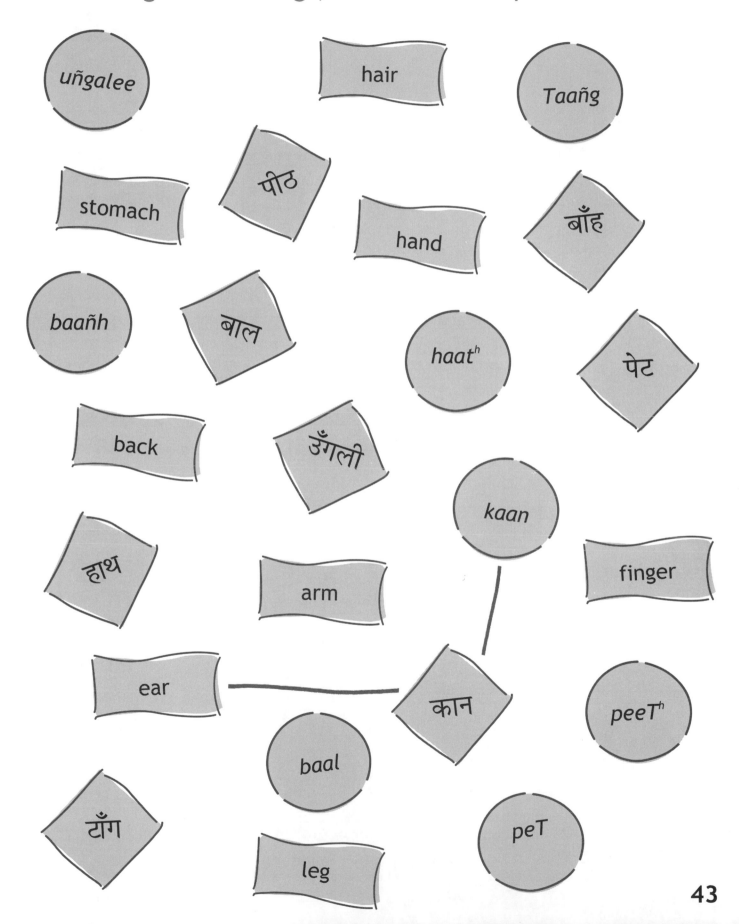

uñgalee

hair

Taañg

stomach

पीठ

hand

बाँह

baañh

बाल

haat[h]

पेट

back

उँगली

kaan

finger

हाथ

arm

ear

कान

peeT[h]

टाँग

baal

peT

leg

43

8 USEFUL EXPRESSIONS

Look at the pictures.
Tear out the flashcards for this topic.
Follow steps 1 and 2 of the plan in the introduction.

कहाँ *kahaañ*

नहीं *naheeñ*

हाँ *haañ*

हैलो *hailo*

गुडबाई
guDbaaee

यहाँ *yahaañ*

कल *kal*

आज *aaj*

कल *kal*

वहाँ *vahaañ*

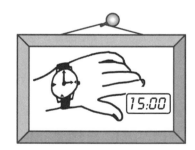

अब *ab*

कितना?
kitnaa

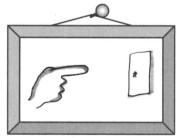

क्षमा कीजिए
kshamaa keejiye

वाह!
vaah

कृपया
kripayaa

धन्यवाद
d^hanyavaad

Match the Hindi words to their English equivalents.

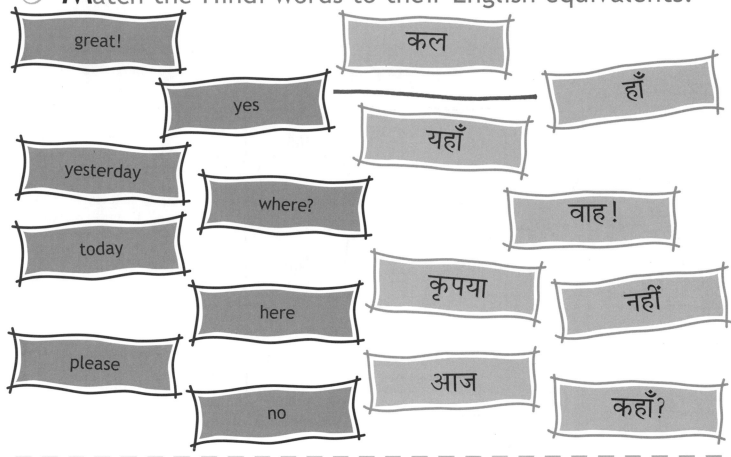

great!

कल

हाँ

yes

यहाँ

yesterday

where?

वाह!

today

here

कृपया

नहीं

please

आज

कहाँ?

no

Now match the Hindi to the pronunciation.

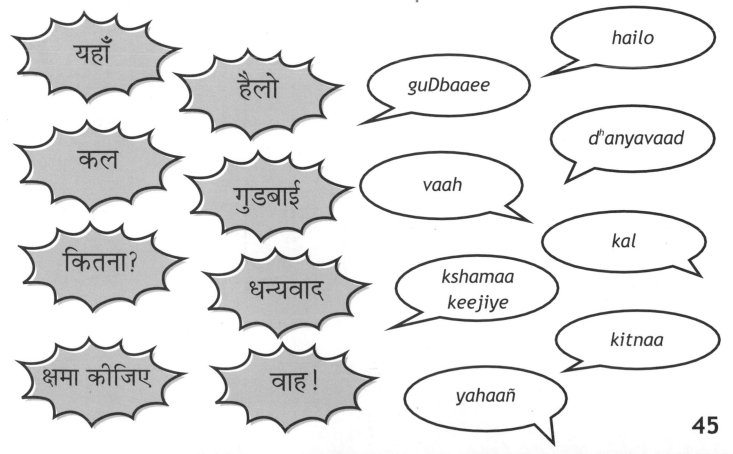

यहाँ

हैलो

hailo

guDbaaee

कल

गुडबाई

dʰanyavaad

vaah

कितना?

धन्यवाद

kal

kshamaa
keejiye

kitnaa

क्षमा कीजिए

वाह!

yahaañ

45

Choose the Hindi word that matches the picture to fill in the English word at the bottom of the page.

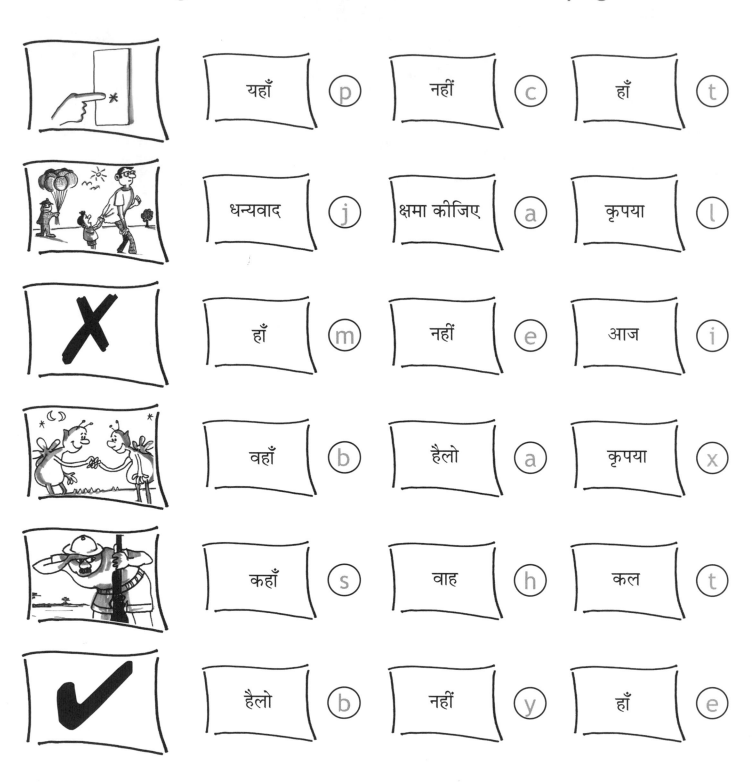

यहाँ (p)	नहीं (c)	हाँ (t)
धन्यवाद (j)	क्षमा कीजिए (a)	कृपया (l)
हाँ (m)	नहीं (e)	आज (i)
वहाँ (b)	हैलो (a)	कृपया (x)
कहाँ (s)	वाह (h)	कल (t)
हैलो (b)	नहीं (y)	हाँ (e)

English word: (p) ( ) ( ) ( ) ( ) ( )

What are these people saying? Write the correct number in each speech bubble, as in the example.

1. हैलो
2. कृपया
3. हाँ
4. नहीं
5. यहाँ
6. क्षमा कीजिए
7. कहाँ?
8. कितना?

47

Finally, match the Hindi words, their pronunciation, and the English meanings, as in the example.

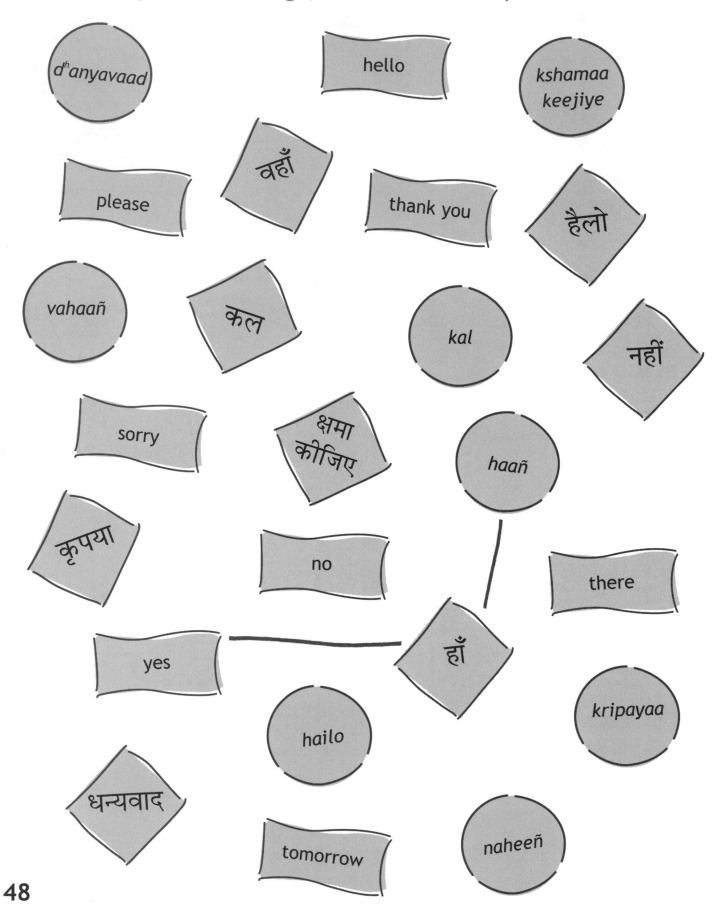

d^hanyavaad

hello

kshamaa keejiye

वहाँ

please

thank you

हैलो

vahaañ

कल

kal

नहीं

sorry

क्षमा कीजिए

haañ

कृपया

no

there

yes

हाँ

kripayaa

hailo

धन्यवाद

tomorrow

naheeñ

● ROUND-UP

This section is designed to review all the 100 words you have met in the different topics. It is a good idea to test yourself with your flashcards before trying this section.

◎ These ten objects are in the picture. Can you find and circle them?

दरवाज़ा	फूल	बिस्तर	कोट	टोपी
साइकिल	कुर्सी	कुत्ता	मछली	जुराब

◎ **S**ee if you can remember all these words.

आज

बस

तेज़

नाक

रेगिस्तान

हाँ

अल्मारी

शेर

ड्रेस

सस्ता

नदी

टाँग

Find the odd one out in these groups of words and say why.

| कुत्ता | गाय | मेज़ | बंदर |

Because it isn't an animal.

- - - - - - - -

| कार | बस | रेलगाड़ी | टेलीफोन |

- - - - - - - -

| फ़ार्म | कोट | कमीज़ | स्कर्ट |

- - - - - - - -

| सागर | झील | नदी | वृक्ष |

- - - - - - - -

| महँगा | गंदा | साफ़ | सिनेमा |

- - - - - - - -

| ख़रगोश | बिल्ली | मछली | शेर |

- - - - - - - -

| बाँह | सोफ़ा | सिर | पेट |

- - - - - - - -

| कृपया | कल | कल | आज |

- - - - - - - -

| चूल्हा | बिस्तर | अल्मारी | फ्रिज |

◎ **L**ook at the objects below for 30 seconds.

◎ **C**over the picture and try to remember all the objects.
Circle the Hindi words for those you remember.

फूल　　　　　जूता　　　　　धन्यवाद　　　दरवाज़ा

कार　　　　　　　यहाँ　　　　कोट　　　　रेलगाड़ी
　　　नहीं

पेटी　　　　　पहाड़　　　　　कुर्सी　　　　घोड़ा

जुर्राब　　　　टी शर्ट　　　　आँख　　　　बिस्तर

निक्कर　　　टैक्सी　　　　टेलीविज़न　　　बंदर

Now match the Hindi words, their pronunciation, and the English meanings, as in the example.

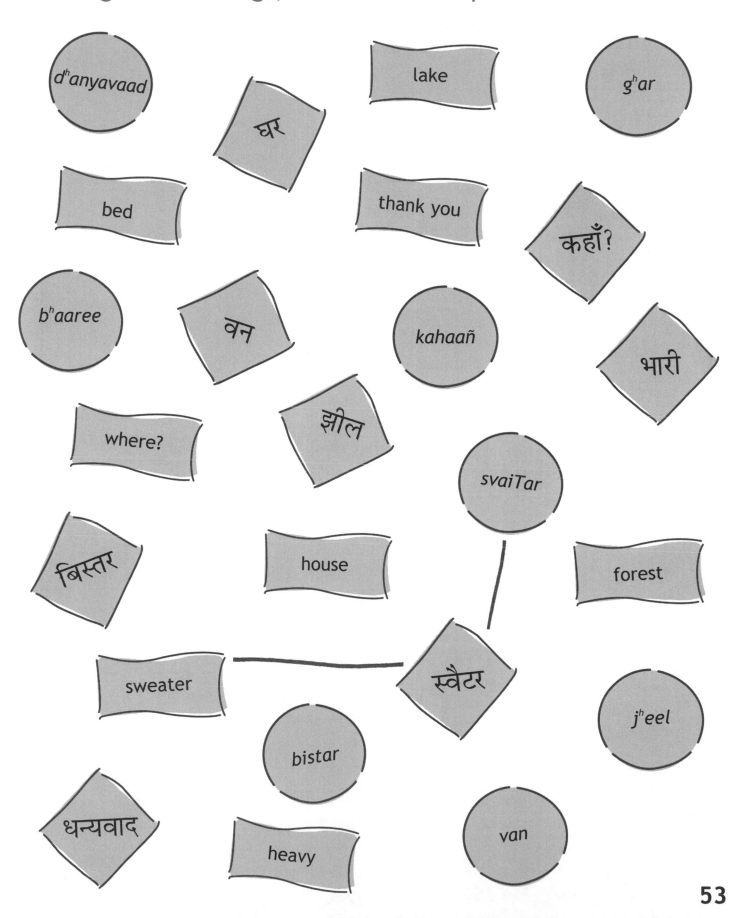

d^hanyavaad

lake

g^har

घर

bed

thank you

कहाँ?

b^haaree

वन

kahaañ

भारी

where?

झील

svaiTar

बिस्तर

house

forest

sweater

स्वैटर

j^heel

bistar

धन्यवाद

van

heavy

Fill in the English phrase at the bottom of the page.

सोफ़ा (w)	टैक्सी (g)	कान (t)
कोट (o)	गंदा (a)	पुल (e)
हाँ (m)	कितना (l)	आज (i)
गाय (b)	खिड़की (l)	रेस्टोरेंट (h)
कहाँ (e)	मुँह (a)	कुत्ता (d)
आँख (o)	मेज़ (p)	हैलो (v)
पहाड़ी (n)	नहीं (y)	बस (r)
ख़रगोश (n)	सड़क (e)	चूल्हा (s)

54 English phrase:  w ◯ ◯ ◯ ◯ ◯ ◯ ◯ !

Look at the two pictures and check (✔) the objects that are different in Picture B.

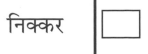 निक्कर

 टी शर्ट

 दरवाज़ा

 बिल्ली

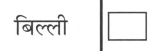 कुर्सी

 मछली

 जुराब

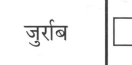 कुत्ता

Picture A

Picture B

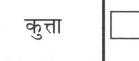

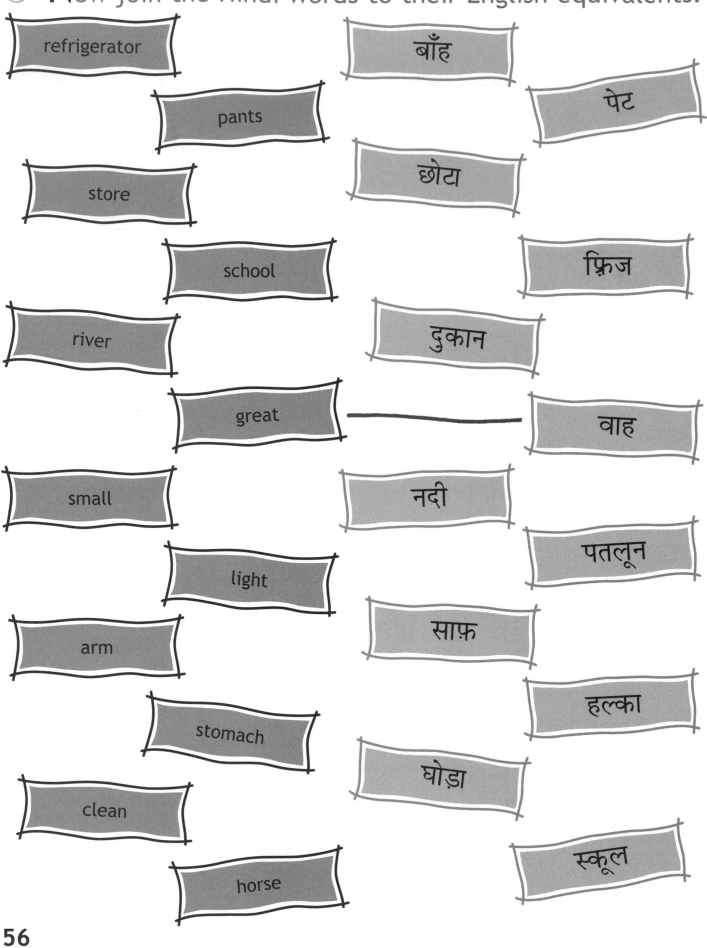

Now join the Hindi words to their English equivalents.

refrigerator

बाँह

पेट

pants

छोटा

store

फ़्रिज

school

दुकान

river

great ———————— वाह

small

नदी

light

पतलून

arm

साफ़

हल्का

stomach

घोड़ा

clean

स्कूल

horse

56

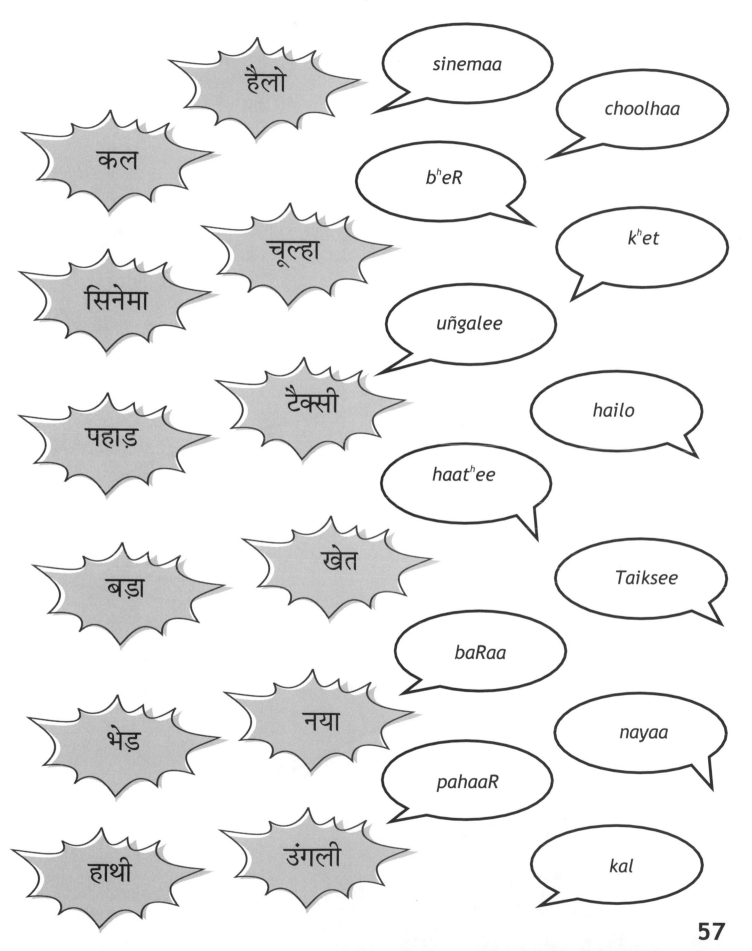

◎ Snake game

● You will need a die and counter(s). You can challenge yourself to reach the finish or play with someone else. You have to throw the exact number to finish.

● Throw the die and move forward that number of spaces. When you land on a word you must pronounce it and say what it means in English. If you can't, you have to go back to the square you came from.

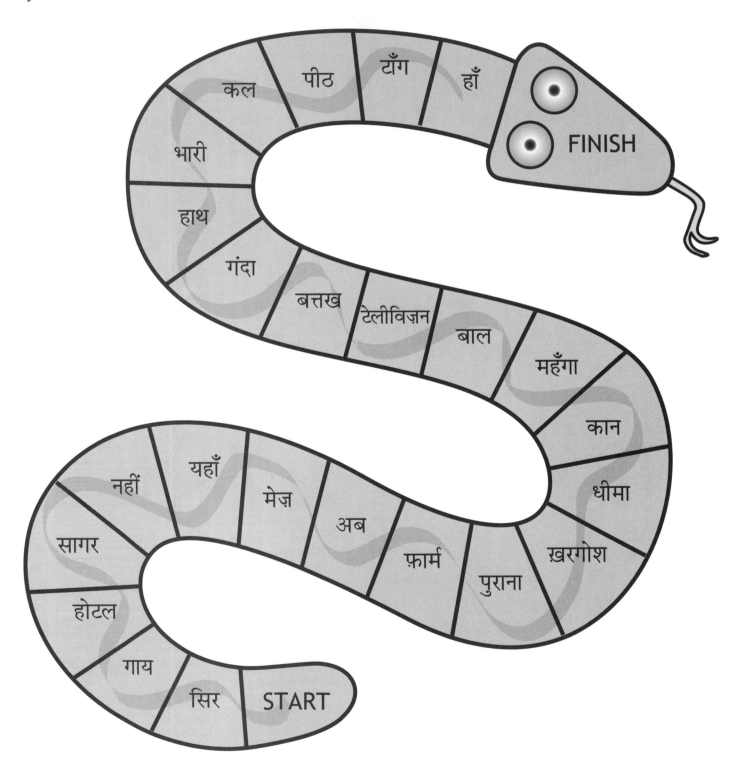

◎ Answers

❶ AROUND THE HOME

Page 10 (top)

See page 9 for correct picture.

Page 10 (bottom)

door	दरवाज़ा
cupboard	अल्मारी
stove	चूल्हा
bed	बिस्तर
table	मेज़
chair	कुर्सी
refrigerator	फ्रिज
computer	कंप्यूटर

Page 11 (top)

मेज़	*mez*
अल्मारी	*almaaree*
कंप्यूटर	*kampyooTar*
बिस्तर	*bistar*
खिड़की	*kʰiRkee*
टेलीफ़ोन	*Taileefon*
टेलीविज़न	*Teleevizan*
कुर्सी	*kursee*

Page 11 (bottom)

Page 12

Page 13

English word: window

❷ CLOTHES

Page 15 (top)

ड्रेस	*Dres*
निक्कर	*nikkar*
जूता	*jootaa*
पेटी	*peTee*
कमीज़	*kameez*
टी शर्ट	*Tee sharT*
टोपी	*Topee*
जुराब	*jurraab*

Page 15 (bottom)

Page 16

hat	टोपी	*Topee*
shoe	जूता	*jootaa*
sock	जुराब	*jurraab*
shorts	निक्कर	*nikkar*
t-shirt	टी शर्ट	*Tee sharT*
belt	पेटी	*peTee*
coat	कोट	*koT*
pants	पतलून	*patloon*

Page 17

टोपी (hat)	2
कोट (coat)	0
पेटी (belt)	2
जूता (shoe)	2 (1 pair)
पतलून (pants)	0
निक्कर (shorts)	2
ड्रेस (dress)	1
जुराब (sock)	6 (3 pairs)
स्कर्ट (skirt)	1
टी शर्ट (t-shirt)	3
कमीज़ (shirt)	0
स्वैटर (sweater)	1

Page 18

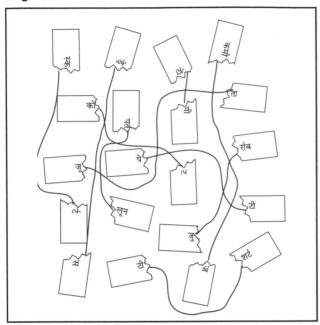

❸ AROUND TOWN

Page 20 (top)

movie theater	सिनेमा
store	दुकान
hotel	होटल
taxi	टैक्सी
car	कार
train	रेलगाड़ी
school	स्कूल
house	घर

Page 20 (bottom)

bicycle	4
taxi	7
house	2
train	6
bus	1
road	3
car	5

Page 21

Page 22

English word: school

Page 23

बस	*bas*
टैक्सी	*Taiksee*
स्कूल	*skool*
कार	*kaar*
होटल	*hoTal*
घर	*g^{h}ar*
साइकिल	*saaikil*
रेलगाड़ी	*relgaree*
दुकान	*dukaan*
सिनेमा	*sinemaa*
रेस्टोरेंट	*restorent*
सड़क	*saRak*

❹ COUNTRYSIDE

Page 25

See page 24 for correct pictures.

Page 26

पुल	✔	खेत	✔
वृक्ष	✔	वन	✔
रेगिस्तान	✘	झील	✘
पहाड़ी	✔	नदी	✔
पहाड़	✔	फूल	✔
सागर	✘	फ़ार्म	✘

Page 27 (top)

पहाड़	*pahaaR*
नदी	*nadee*
वन	*van*
रेगिस्तान	*registaan*
सागर	*saagar*
फ़ार्म	*faarm*
पुल	*pul*
खेत	*k^{h}et*

Page 27 (bottom)

झी	म	क	ग	पु	फू	ट	स
र	पु	व	वृ	ल	झी	ष	क्ष
फु	स	फू	क्ष	ड्रा	ल	वृ	र
त	पु	र	श	भ	फा	ख	झी
ट	र	ल	ला	थ	र्म	क्ष	पु
प	हा	ड़ी	लू	वृ	ल	फू	ल
ढ़	य	रू	झी	सी	व	ह	झ
ढ	वृ	घ	झी	ल	ण	क्ष	थ

Page 28

sea	सागर	*saagar*
lake	झील	*jʰeel*
desert	रेगिस्तान	*registaan*
farm	फ़ार्म	*faarm*
flower	फूल	*pʰool*
mountain	पहाड़	*pahaaR*
river	नदी	*nadee*
field	खेत	*kʰet*

❺ OPPOSITES

Page 30

expensive	महँगा
big	बड़ा
light	हल्का
slow	धीमा
clean	साफ़
inexpensive	सस्ता
dirty	गंदा
small	छोटा
heavy	भारी
new	नया
fast	तेज़
old	पुराना

Page 31

English word: change

Page 32

Odd one outs are those which are not opposites:

भारी

छोटा

नया

गंदा

धीमा

सस्ता

Page 33

old	नया
big	छोटा
new	पुराना
slow	तेज़
dirty	साफ़
small	बड़ा
heavy	हल्का
clean	गंदा
light	भारी
expensive	सस्ता
inexpensive	महँगा

❻ ANIMALS

Page 35

गाय   ख़रगोश   मछली   शेर

भेड़   कुत्ता   बंदर

घोड़ा   चूहा   बिल्ली

Page 36

ख़रगोश	*khargosh*
घोड़ा	*gʰoRaa*
बंदर	*bandar*
कुत्ता	*kuttaa*
बिल्ली	*billee*
चूहा	*choohaa*
बत्तख	*battakʰ*
मछली	*machʰalee*
शेर	*sher*
भेड़	*bʰeR*
गाय	*gaay*
हाथी	*haatʰee*

Page 37

elephant	✔	mouse	✘
monkey	✘	cat	✔
sheep	✔	dog	✘
lion	✔	cow	✔
fish	✔	horse	✘
duck	✘	rabbit	✔

Page 38

monkey	बंदर
cow	गाय
mouse	चूहा
dog	कुत्ता
sheep	भेड़
fish	मछली
lion	शेर
elephant	हाथी
cat	बिल्ली
duck	बत्तख
rabbit	ख़रगोश
horse	घोड़ा

❼ PARTS OF THE BODY

Page 40

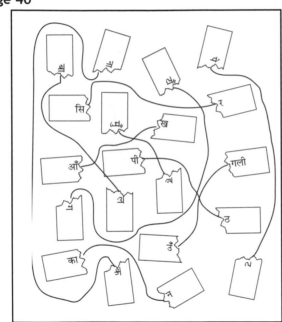

Page 41 (top)

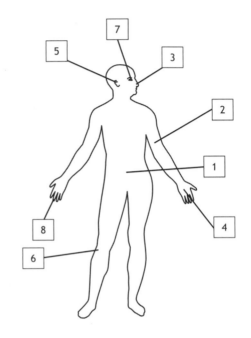

You should have also drawn pictures of:

leg; mouth; ear; nose; eye; hair

Page 41 (bottom)

सिर	sir
कान	kaan
पेट	peT
नाक	naak
बाँह	baañh
मुँह	muñh
आँख	aañk^h
पीठ	peeT^h

Page 42

1 पेट	peT
2 बाँह	baañh
3 नाक	naak
4 हाथ	haat^h
5 कान	kaan
6 टाँग	Taañg
7 आँख	aañk^h
8 उँगली	uñgalee

Page 43

ear	कान	kaan
hair	बाल	baal
hand	हाथ	haat^h
stomach	पेट	peT
arm	बाँह	baañh
back	पीठ	peeT^h
finger	उँगली	uñgalee
leg	टाँग	Taañg

⑧ USEFUL EXPRESSIONS

Page 45 (top)

great!	वाह!
yes	हाँ
yesterday	कल
where?	कहाँ?
today	आज
here	यहाँ
please	कृपया
no	नहीं

Page 45 (bottom)

यहाँ	*yahaañ*
हैलो	*hailo*
कल	*kal*
गुडबाई	*guDbaaee*
कितना?	*kitnaa*
धन्यवाद	*dʰanyavaad*
क्षमा कीजिए	*kshamaa keejiye*
वाह!	*vaah*

Page 46

English word: please

Page 47

Page 48

yes	हाँ	*haañ*
hello	हैलो	*hailo*
no	नहीं	*naheeñ*
sorry	क्षमा कीजिए	*kshamaa keejiye*
please	कृपया	*kripayaa*
there	वहाँ	*vahaañ*
thank you	धन्यवाद	*dʰanyavaad*
tomorrow	कल	*kal*

● ROUND-UP

Page 49

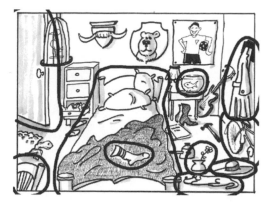

Page 50

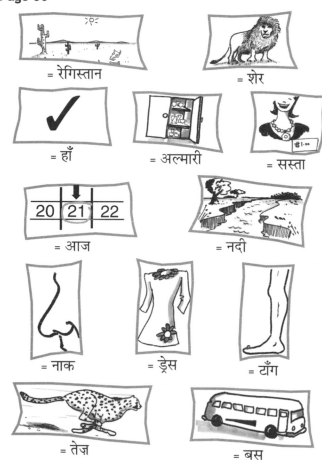

= रेगिस्तान   = शेर

= हाँ   = अल्मारी   = सस्ता

= आज   = नदी

= नाक   = ड्रेस   = टाँग

= तेज़   = बस

Page 51

मेज़ (Because it isn't an animal.)

टेलीफ़ोन (Because it isn't a means of transport.)

फ़ार्म (Because it isn't an item of clothing.)

वृक्ष (Because it isn't connected with water.)

सिनेमा (Because it isn't a descriptive word.)

मछली (Because it lives in water/doesn't have legs.)

सोफ़ा (Because it isn't a part of the body.)

कृपया (Because it isn't an expression of time.)

बिस्तर (Because you wouldn't find it in the kitchen.)

63

Page 52

Words that appear in the picture:

टी शर्ट
कार
फूल
जूता
रेल गाड़ी
बंदर
टेलीविज़न
कुर्सी
पेटी
निक्कर

Page 53

sweater	स्वैटर	*savaiTar*
lake	झील	*jʰeel*
thank you	धन्यवाद	*dʰanyavaad*
bed	बिस्तर	*bistar*
house	घर	*gʰar*
forest	वन	*van*
where?	कहाँ	*kahaañ*
heavy	भारी	*bʰaaree*

Page 54

English phrase: well done!

Page 55

निक्कर	✔ (shade)
टी शर्ट	✗
दरवाज़ा	✔ (handle)
बिल्ली	✗
कुर्सी	✔ (back)
मछली	✔ (direction)
जुराब	✔ (pattern)
कुत्ता	✗

Page 56

refrigerator	फ्रिज
pants	पतलून
store	दुकान
school	स्कूल
river	नदी
great	वाह
small	छोटा
light	हल्का
arm	बाँह
stomach	पेट
clean	साफ़
horse	घोड़ा

Page 57

हैलो	*hailo*
कल	*kal*
चूल्हा	*choolhaa*
सिनेमा	*sinema*
टैक्सी	*Taiksee*
पहाड़	*pahaaR*
खेत	*kʰet*
बड़ा	*baRaa*
नया	*nayaa*
भेड़	*bʰeR*
उँगली	*uñgalee*
हाथी	*haatʰee*

Page 58

Here are the English equivalents of the word, in order from START to FINISH:

head	*sir*	expensive	*mahañgaa*
cow	*gaay*	hair	*baal*
hotel	*hoTal*	television	*Teleevizan*
sea	*saagar*	duck	*battakʰ*
no	*naheeñ*	dirty	*gandaa*
here	*yahaañ*	hand	*haatʰ*
table	*mez*	heavy	*bʰaaree*
now	*ab*	tomorrow	*kal*
farm	*faarm*	back	*peeTʰ*
old	*puranaa*	leg	*Taañg*
rabbit	*khargosh*	yes	*haañ*
slow	*dʰeemaa*		
ear	*kaan*		

64

कंप्यूटर

kampyooTar

खिड़की

kʰiRkee

मेज़

mez

अल्मारी

almaaree

फ़्रिज

frij

कुर्सी

kursee

सोफ़ा

sofaa

चूल्हा

choolha

दरवाज़ा

darvaazaa

बिस्तर

bistar

टेलीफ़ोन

Taileefon

टेलीविज़न

Teleevizan

window	computer
cupboard	table
chair	refrigerator
stove	sofa
bed	door
television	telephone

पेटी *peTee*	कोट *koT*
स्कर्ट *skarT*	टोपी *Topee*
टी शर्ट *Tee sharT*	जूता *jootaa*
स्वैटर *savaiTar*	कमीज़ *kameez*
निक्कर *nikkar*	जुर्राब *jurraab*
पतलून *patloon*	ड्रेस *Dres*

coat	belt
hat	skirt
shoe	t-shirt
shirt	sweater
sock	shorts
dress	pants

स्कूल	कार
skool	*kaar*
सड़क	सिनेमा
saRak	*sinemaa*
होटल	दुकान
hoTal	*dukaan*
टैक्सी	साइकिल
Taiksee	*saaikil*
रेस्टोरेंट	बस
restorent	*bas*
रेलगाड़ी	घर
relgaRee	*ghar*

car	school
movie theater	road
store	hotel
bicycle	taxi
bus	restaurant
house	train

झील	वन
jʰeel	*van*
पहाड़ी	सागर
pahaaRee	*saagar*
पहाड़	वृक्ष
pahaaR	*vriksh*
रेगिस्तान	फूल
registaan	*pʰool*
पुल	नदी
pul	*nadee*
फ़ार्म	खेत
faarm	*kʰet*

forest	lake
sea	hill
tree	mountain
flower	desert
river	bridge
field	farm

भारी

bʰaaree

हल्का

halkaa

बड़ा

baRaa

छोटा

chʰoTaa

पुराना

puraanaa

नया

nayaa

तेज़

tez

धीमा

dʰeemaa

साफ़

saaf

गंदा

gandaa

सस्ता

sastaa

महँगा

mahañgaa

light	heavy
small	big
new	old
slow	fast
dirty	clean
expensive	inexpensive

बत्तख

battakh

बिल्ली

billee

चूहा

choohaa

गाय

gaay

ख़रगोश

khargosh

कुत्ता

kuttaa

घोड़ा

gʰoRaa

बंदर

bandar

शेर

sher

मछली

machʰalee

हाथी

haatʰee

भेड़

bʰeR

cat	duck
cow	mouse
dog	rabbit
monkey	horse
fish	lion
sheep	elephant

बाँह

baañh

उँगली

uñgalee

सिर

sir

मुँह

mooñh

कान

kaan

टाँग

Taañg

हाथ

haat^h

पेट

peT

आँख

aañk^h

बाल

baal

नाक

naak

पीठ

peeT^h

finger	arm
mouth	head
leg	ear
stomach	hand
hair	eye
back	nose